FIFTIES THE

Published by
EMI Music Publishing Limited/Music Sales Limited

Exclusive distributors:
Music Sales Limited, 78 Newman Street,
London W1P 3LA, England.

EMI Music Publishing Limited,
138-140 Charing Cross Road,
London WC2H 0LD, England.

Designed by Ken Carroll.
Text Edited by Jonathon Green.
Art Directed by Pearce Marchbank.

ISBN 0.86001.243.3
AM 19712

X 3.50

CONTENTS

Best Wishes
Elvis Presley

PRESLEY injected movements of the tongue and indulged in wordless singing that was singularly distasteful. When Presley executes his bumps and grinds it must be remembered by the Columbia Broadcasting System that even a 12-year-old's curiosity may be over stimulated.'——
——JACK GOULD, 'The New York Times' ——

WHEN you put on a uniform there are certain
—inhibitions which you must accept.—
—DWIGHT D. EISENHOWER—

SINCERITY is the quality that comes through on
————————— television. —————————
———— RICHARD M. NIXON ————

AMERICA, I'm putting my queer shoulder to the
———————— wheel.————————
——— ALLEN GINSBERG, 'America' ———

JIMMY PORTER: 'Hallelujah, I'm alive! I've an idea. Why don't we have a little game? Let's pretend we're actually alive. Just for a while. What do —— you say? Let's pretend we're human. ——
—— JOHN OSBORNE, 'Look Back In Anger' ——

REDS just aren't the kind who can stand a big push. Like it or not, they are still a bunch of lousy peasants who can be knocked into shape by the likes of us. They're shouting slobs who'll run like hell when class shows and they know this inside their ———— feeble heads. ————
———— MICKEY SPILLANE, 'The Girl Hunters' ————

YOU'VE never had it so good.
—— HAROLD ——
—— MACMILLAN ——

█T was Tuesday, January 11th. It was cool in Los
Angeles. We were working the Day watch out of
Forgery Division. My partner's Frank Smith. The
—— boss is Captain Welch. My name's Friday.——
—— JACK WEBB in 'Dragnet', NBC-TV ——

WE will bury you!
— NIKITA —
— KRUSCHEV —

QUESTIONER : When did you discover Communism?
SEN. McCARTHY : Why, about two and a
half months ago.

WE'VE done the bugger.
— SHERPA —
— TENSING —

I'D rather be fat than famous.
— JACK KEROUAC —

THE trouble with censors is that they worry if a girl has cleavage. They ought to worry if she hasn't any.
— MARILYN MONROE —

WE are not at war with Egypt – we are in an armed
conflict.
—— ANTHONY EDEN, on Suez ——

THE ability to get to the verge without getting into war is the necessary art. If you cannot master it, you inevitably get into war. If you try to run away from it, if you are scared to go to the brink, you are ───────── lost. ─────────
─── JOHN FOSTER DULLES ───

AWORLD without policemen would be a world
———————— without music. ————————
———————DANIEL J. SHIELDS,———————
Mayor of Johnstown, Pennsylvania

SOON there will be only five kings left: the Kings of England, Diamonds, Hearts, Spades and Clubs.
———— KING FAROUK ————

HOW to fold a diaper depends on the size of the baby and the diaper.
———— DR. SPOCK ————

ALLENTOWN JAIL

Words and Music by: Irving Gordon

free, Nev er go free,_____ 'Cause he stole a
wrong, For can't you see,_____ My love stole a
town, For can't you see,_____ My love stole a

dia-mond, a beau-ti-ful dia-mond, To give,__ to give to me.__
dia-mond, a beau-ti-ful dia-mond, To give,__ to give to me.__
dia-mond, a beau-ti-ful dia-mond, To prove__ his love to me.__

REFRAIN

Some-where in Al - len - town Jail,_____ My heart waits in

Al - len - town Jail._____ 2. I'll Jail._____
3. You'll

ANSWER ME

English Words by: Carl Sigman
Music by: Gerhard Winkler and Fred Rauch

(Shouted) Answer me!

An-swer me oh, my love Just what sin have I been guilt-y of ___ Tell me how I came to lose your love Please an-swer me ___ my love ___ You were mine yes-ter-day I be-lieved that love was here to stay Won't you tell me where I've gone a-stray Please

29

AM I THAT EASY TO FORGET?

Words and Music by : Carl Belew and W. S. Stevenson

How could you leave with-out re-gret? AM I THAT EA-SY TO FOR-GET?

Eb   Bb7   Eb   Ab

Be-fore you leave, be sure you find ____ you want { her / his } love much

Eb   Eb7   Ab

more than mine ____ 'Cause I'll just say we've nev-er met ____ If I'm that ea-sy to for-

Eb   Bbm7   Eb7   Ab   Bb7

1

get.   *tacet*   They say you've found some-bod-y

2

get. ____

Eb   Cdim   Bb7   Eb   Ab   Eb   E7   Eb

A BEAUTIFUL FRIENDSHIP

Words by : Stanley Styne
Music by : Donald Khan

We were al-ways like sis - ter and bro - ther, un - til to - night when we looked at each oth - er.

That was the end of a BEAU - TI-FUL FRIEND-SHIP and just the be-

1.
gin - ning of love.

2.
love.

ritard.

FROM A JACK TO A KING

Words and Music by: Ned Miller

ETERNALLY

Words by: Geoffrey Parsons and John Turner
Music by: Charles Chaplin

CHORUS

FLY ME TO THE MOON (In Other Words)

Words and Music by: Bart Howard

IF I HAD A HAMMER (The Hammer Song)

Words and Music by : Lee Hays and Pete Seeger

all o - ver this land; I'd ham-mer out dan - ger,
all o - ver this land; I'd ring __ out dan - ger,
all o - ver this land; I'd sing __ out dan - ger,
all o - ver this land; It's the ham-mer of jus - tice,

I'd ham - mer out a warn - ing, __ I'd ham - mer out
I'd ring __ out a warn - ing, __ I'd ring __ out
I'd sing __ out a warn - ing, __ I'd sing __ out
It's the bell __ of __ free - dom, __ It's the song a - bout

love be - tween all of my broth-ers, All _____ o - ver this
love be - tween all of my broth-ers, All _____ o - ver this
love be - tween all of my broth-ers, All _____ o - ver this
love be - tween all of my broth-ers, All _____ o - ver this

1.2.3.
land. _____ **2.** If I had a
land. _____ **3.** If I had a
land. _____ **4.** Well I got a

4.
land. _____

IN THE WEE SMALL HOURS OF THE MORNING

Words by: Bob Hilliard
Music by: David Mann

sleep, You lie a-wake and think a-bout the girl, And nev-er ev-er think of count-ing (boy,)

sheep. When your lone-ly heart has learned its les-son You'd be hers if on-ly she would (his) (he)

call. IN THE WEE SMALL HOURS OF THE MORNING That's the time you miss her most of (him)

all. IN THE time you miss her most of all. (him)

molto rit.

43

JAILHOUSE ROCK

Words and Music by: Jerry Leiber and Mike Stoller

should-'ve heard those knocked - out jail - birds sing._ ⎫
whole ___ rhy - thm sec - tion was the pur - ple gang._ ⎬ Let's rock!
on and do the Jail - house Rock with me."_ ⎭

F (Tacet)

Bb7

Let's rock!

Ev-'ry - bo - dy in the whole cell block_

F

C7   C7 sus 4

1-2   3

___ was a dan - cin' to the Jail-house Rock!_   ___

Bb7   F   Bb7   F   E

EXTRA CHORUSES

4. The sad sack was a-sittin' on a block of stone,
   Way over in the corner weeping all alone.
   The warden said, "Hey buddy, don't you be no square,
   If you can't find a partner, use a wooden chair!"
   Let's rock, etc.

5. Shifty Henry said to Bugs, "For Heaven's sake,
   No one s lookin', now's our chance to make a break."
   Bugsy turned to Shifty and he said, "Nix, nix,
   I wanna stick around a while and get my kicks,"
   Let's rock, etc.

LOVE ME TENDER

Words and Music by: Elvis Presley and Vera Matson

life com - plete,   And I   love you   so.
I   be - long,   And we'll nev - er   part.
all the years,   Till the end   of   time.
fol - low you   Ev - 'ry - where you go .

A7   D7   D7   G
          sus4

CHORUS

Love me ten - der, love me true,   All my dreams ful -

G   B7   Em   G7   C   Cm

- fill   For, my dar - lin',   I   love you,

G   G   Dm6 E7+ E7   A7

And I al - ways will.   And I al - ways will.

D7   D7   G   Am7 D7   D7   D7   G
sus4   sus4

ALL THE WAY

Words by: Sammy Cahn
Music by: James Van Heusen

That's how it's got to feel; Deep - er _____ than the

deep blue sea is, that's how deep it goes, __ if it's real.

When some-bod - y needs you, it's no good un-less {he}{she} needs you ALL THE

WAY. Through the good or lean years and for all the in be - tween years,

MILORD

Original Words by: G. Moustaki
Music by: Marguerite Monnot
Words by: Bunny Lewis

-bye" That South-ern Belle Mi Lord has got a heart of ice Love can be hell Mi Lord as
-gret. So let her go Mi-Lord come on re-lax be smart 'Cos if you don't you know she'll

C7 C13 Db9 C13 F° F F° F Bb F

VERSE
Fminor

well as Par - a - dise. You met her at a Ball her lips were rub-y red, Her
on-ly break your heart. The sto-ry is the same when ev er young love grows, And

Gm7 C7 F Fm C+ Fm C+

laz-y South-ern drawl soon turn'd your no-ble head, You swore you'd nev-er part tho' you lived far a -
no one is to blame it's just the way it goes, You're not the first who's found that love can be un-

Fm Eb Fm C+ Fm Eb

- way How could you know her heart Like oth-er hearts would stray _____ Come on, get
- kind And still the world goes round But one hearts left be - hind _____ Come on, get

Db C Db C7 (♭9)

52

Hip, Mi-Lord and let life rip Mi-Lord Be sure there's plent-y more of

lov-ing to be done There's chicks to meet Mi-Lord with lips as sweet Mi-Lord And hearts to

make and break be-fore the race is run, So hit the town Mi-Lord come on and

be my guest, We'll turn it up-side down and dev-il take the rest. Come on, get rest.

NON DIMENTICAR

English Words by : Shelley Dobbins
Italian Words by : Michele Galdieri
Music by : P. G. Redi

here._____ Please do not for - get that our lips have met and I've held you tight dear,
cuor._____ Se ci se-pa - rò, se ci al-lon - ta - nò l'a - la del de - sti - no,__

Bb   Ebm6   Bbdim   Bb7   Fm7   Bb7   Fm7   Bb7   Bb+7   Eb   Ebmaj7

Was   it dreams a - go   my heart felt this glow, or on - ly just to-night dear?__
non ne ho col - pa, no,   e mi sen - ti - ro   sem-pre a te vi - ci - no.

Eb6   Gm7   C7   Gm7   C7   Cm7   Ebm6   F7

Non Di-men-ti - car al-though you trav-el far, my dar - ling,___ It's my heart you own, so I'll wait a -
Non di-men-ti - car che t'ho vo-lu-to tan-to be - ne ___ For-se nel mio cuor puoi tro-va-re an-

Bb   Bbmaj7   Bb   G9   Cm7   F7   Bdim   Cm7   F9   Cm7

1   **2**

- lone   Non Di-men-ti - car.   - car. _____
- cor   tan-to e tan-to a - mor.   - mor. _____

rall.

F9   Cm7   Ebm   F9b   Bb   Gm7   Cm7   F11   F9b   Bb   Eb   Ebm   Bb

RAVE ON

Words and Music by: Sunny West,
Bill Tilghman and Norman Petty

RELEASE ME

Words and Music by: Eddie Miller, Dub Williams,
Robert Young and Robert Harris

Moderato, with feeling

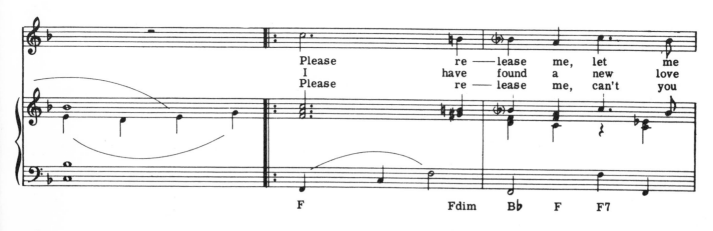

Please re—lease me, let me
I have found a new love
Please re—lease me, can't love you

go dear, for I don't
and you'd be
see, I will a

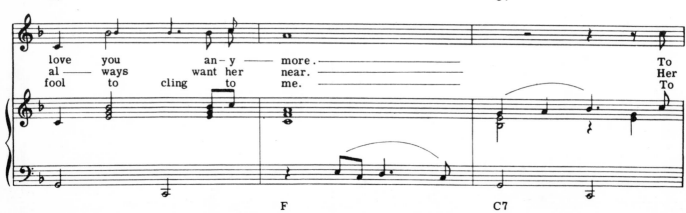

love you an—y—more. To
al—ways want her near. Her
fool to cling to me. To

waste   our   lives   would   be   a   sin,
lips   are   a   warm   while   yours   are   cold,
live   a   lie   would   bring   us   pain,

re——lease me   and   let   me   love a
re——lease me   my   dar—ling   let me
so   re—lease me   and   let me   love a——

1. 2.

— gain.
    go.

3.

— gain.

59

THREE COINS IN THE FOUNTAIN

Words by : Sammy Cahn
Music by : Jule Styne

Three coins in the foun-tain, Each one seek-ing hap-pi-ness, Thrown by three hope-ful lov-ers, Which one will the foun-tain bless? Three hearts in the foun-tain, Each heart long-ing for its home, There they lie in the foun-tain Some-where in the heart of

PEGGY SUE

Words and Music by: Jerry Allison, Norman Petty and Buddy Holly

PEG - GY SUE, ___ PEG - GY SUE, ___

Pret-ty, pret-ty, pret-ty, pret-ty, PEG - GY SUE, ___ Oh, my Peg-gy, ___

My PEG - GY SUE; ___ Oh, well, I

love you gal, ___ and I need you, PEG - GY SUE. ___

63

(LOVE IS) THE TENDER TRAP

Words by : Sammy Cahn
Music by : James Van Heusen

hand in hand be-neath the trees ___ And soon there's mu-sic in the breeze, _____ You're act-ing kind of smart, un-til ___ your heart just goes whap! Those trees, ___ that breeze, They're part ___ of THE TEN-DER TRAP! ___ Some star-ry night, when {her}{his} kiss-es make you tin - gle, _____ {She'll}{He'll} hold you tight and you'll hate your-self for be - ing ___ sin - gle. ___ And

all at once it seems so nice, ___ The folks are throw-ing shoes and rice, ___ You

hur-ry to a spot, that's just ___ a dot on the map! You won-

-der how ___ it all ___ came a-bout, It's too ___ late now, there's no ___ get-ting out, You fell ___

in love, And love ___ is THE TEN-DER TRAP!

1.

2. You

UNFORGETTABLE

Words and Music by : Irving Gordon

Un-for-get-ta-ble _____ in ev-'ry way, _____

And for ev-er-more _____ that's how you'll stay. _____ That's why, dar-ling,

it's in-cred-i-ble, That some-one so Un-for-get-ta-ble Thinks that I am

Un-for-get-ta-ble too.

too. _____

AN AFFAIR TO REMEMBER (Our Love Affair)

Words by : Harold Adamson and Leo McCarey
Music by : Harry Warren
French Words by : Tanis Chandler

love af-fair, may it al-ways be a flame to burn through e-
bel a - mour tou-jours gran - dis - sant, Qui dé - fie-ra les é-

F   F°   C   Cm   Gm   C7

-ter - ni - ty. So, take my hand with a fer-vent pray'r, That
-preuves du temps. Trou-vons la joie, res-te dans mes bras, Que

Cm6   D7-9 D7-9 D7   Gm   B♭°   Am7   E   A♭m6
       +5   -5

we may live and we may share a love af - fair to re-
nous vi - vions un bel a - mour, Af - faire de coeur, qu'on n'ou-

Gm7   E♭   Am7   D9   D9 D7   Gm7   Gm6
rall   -5 -9

1   **2**

-mem - ber. Our - ber.
-blie pas. Ce pas.

a tempo   a tempo   poco rit

C7 -9   F   F   F°   Gm7   F

71

AUTUMN CONCERTO

Words by: Paul Siegel, John Turner and Geoffrey Parsons
Music by: C. Bargoni
Italian Lyric by: Danpa

CARA MIA

Words and Music by : Tulio Trapani and Lee Lange

Ca-ra Mi - a why must we say good-bye? Each time we part, my heart wants to die. My dar-ling hear my pray'r, Ca-ra Mi - a fair Here are my arms, you a - lone will share.

CATCH A FALLING STAR

Words and Music by: Paul Vance and Lee Pockriss

THE BRIDGE OF SIGHS

Words and Music by: Billy Reid

VERSE

A lit-tle bridge that leads to love-land,
Where all the lov-ers kiss good-night,
That's where my dear, you'll find me wait-ing,
Wait-ing and hop-ing dear you'll come to me to-night.

CHORUS

C'EST SI BON (It's So Good)

English words by : Jerry Seelen
Music by : Henri Betti
French Words by : Andre Hornez

CHORUS

"C'EST SI BON"_____ Lov-ers say that in France,_____ When they thrill to ro - mance,_____
"C'EST SI BON"_____ De - par - tir n'im porte où,_____ Bras des - sus bras des - sous_____
"C'EST SI BON"_____ De pou voir l'em bras - ser_____ Et puis de r'commen - cer_____

Am7 D7 G Gm Am7

____ It means that it's so good._____ C'EST SI BON,_____ So I say it to you,_____
____ En chan - tant des chan - sons._____ C'EST SI BON,_____ De se dir' des mots doux._____
____ A la moindre oc - ca - sion._____ C'EST SI BON,_____ De jou - er du pia - no._____

D7 G D7+ G Am7 D7 G

____ Like the French people do,_____ Be - cause it's oh, so good._____ Ev - 'ry word, ev - 'ry
____ Des pe - tits riens du tout_____ Mais qui en di - sent long._____ En voy - ant no - tre
____ Tout le long de son dos_____ Tan dis que nous dan - sons._____ C'est i - noui ce qu'elle

Gm Am7 D7 G Bb7 Eb

sigh, ev - 'ry kiss, dear,_____ Leads to on - ly one thought and it's this,_____ dear. It's so
mi - ne ra - vi - e_____ Les pas - sant dans la rue, nous en - vient._____ C'EST SI
a pour sé - dui - re,_____ Sans par - ler de c'que je n'peux pas dire._____ C'EST SI

Ab Eb A7 A'm7 Eb9 D7

good, _____ No - thing else can re - place, _____ Just your slight - est em brace. _____
BON, _____ De guet - ter dans ses yeux _____ Un es - poir mer veil - leux. _____
BON, _____ Quand j'la tiens dans mes bras, _____ De me dir' que tout ça _____

Am7   D7   G   Gm Am7

_ And if you on - ly would, _____ be my own, _____ For the rest of my
_ Qui don - ne le fris - son. _____ C'EST SI BON, _____ Ces pe - tit's sen sa -
_ C'est à moi pour de bon. _____ C'EST SI BON, _____ Et si nous nous ai -

D7   Dm6   E7   Bbm7 Am7   Cm

1.

days. _____ I will whis - per this phrase, _____ My dar - ling, "C'EST SI BON" _____ C'EST SI
- tions. _____ Ça vaut mieux qu'un mil - lion. _____ Tell'ment, tell 'ment c'est bon. _____ C'EST SI
- mons. _____ Cher - chez pas la rai - son _____ C'est parc' que "C'EST SI BON" _____ C'EST SI

G   Ab7   D7   G   D9 G

2.

_____ I mean that it's so good, _____ When I say "C'EST SI BON!" _____ And I say "C'EST SI BON!"

G   D7   G   D7   G   D7

Be - cause it's oh, so good. _____

G   D7   G   Ab9 G6   83

CRY

Words and Music by : Churchill Kohlman

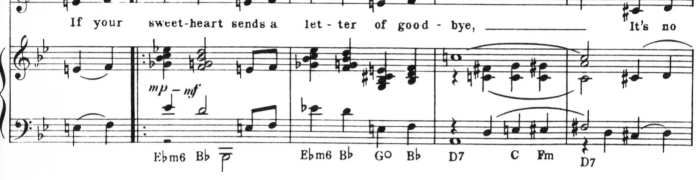

If your sweet-heart sends a let-ter of good-bye, _____ It's no

se-cret you'll feel bet-ter if you cry _____ When wak-ing from a

bad dream don't you some-times think it's real? But it's on-ly false e-

EBB TIDE

Words by : Carl Sigman
Music by : Robert Maxwell

87

THE GREEN DOOR

Words by: Marvin Moore
Music by: Bob Davie

Don't know what they're do-in' but they laugh a lot be-hind the Green Door.
When I said, "Joe sent me," some-one laughed out loud be-hind the Green Door.

Wish they'd let me in so I could find out what's be-hind the Green Door.
All I want to do is join the hap-py crowd be-hind the

Green Door. Mid - night, one more night with-out sleep-in'!

Watch-in' till the morn-ing comes creep-in'! Green Door, what's the se-cret you're

keep - in'? Green Door, what's the se-cret you're keep-in'? Green Door!

HI-LILI, HI-LO

Words by: Helen Deutsch
Music by: Bronislau Kaper

A song of love is a song of woe, don't ask me how I know.

A song of love is a sad song, for I have loved and it's so. I sit at the win-dow and watch the rain, Hi-Li-li, Hi-Li-li, Hi-Lo. To-mor-row I'll prob-a-bly love a-gain, Hi-Li-li, Hi-Li-li, Hi-Lo. A -Li-li, Hi-Li-li Hi-Lo.

91

HIGH NOON

Words by: Ned Washington
Music by: Dimitri Tiomkin

I do not know what fate a - waits me

Eb   Fm7/ Eb
      Bb

I on - ly know I must be brave

Eb7   Ab   C7

And I must face a man who hates me   or lie a

Fm   F#o   Eb   Eb7   Ab

cow-ard,   A cra-ven cow-ard,   Or lie a cow - ard

Eb   Ab   Eb   Ab   Eb

leave   me?   Do not for-sake me, oh my dar-lin'____

____   You made that prom-ise as   a   bride____

Do   not for - sake me, oh my   dar - lin',____   Although you're

griev-in',   don't think of leav-in'   now that I need   you

by my side!_____ side!_____

Wait a - long_____ wait a - long___

Fm7   Bb7   Eb   Fm7   Eb

Ab   Eb

wait a-long_____ wait a - long_____

Ab   Eb

dim.   8va - - - - - - - - -

rall._____   pp

KISSES SWEETER THAN WINE

Words by : Paul Campbell
Music by : Joel Newman

she had___ kiss-es sweet-er than wine___ She had um, um___

Em   Bm7   Em   B7   Em

kiss-es sweet-er than wine_____ sweet-er than wine._____ 2.Well I

Bm7   Em   Bm7   Em   B7

asked her to mar - ry and be my sweet wife,_ I told her
worked ve - ry hard both___ me and my wife,_ A - work - ing
chil - dren they num - ber___ just a - bout four___ And they
now that I'm old and I'm read - y to go__ I get to

Em   Am   Em

we'd be so hap-py for the rest of our life. I begged her and I plead - ed like a
hand in hand___ to have a good life. We had corn___ in the field___ and___
all had a sweet-heart a-knock-ing at the door They all___ got___ mar - ried and they
think-ing what hap - pened a long time a - go. Had a lot___ of___ kids, a lot of

Am   Bm7   Em   Am

nat - u - ral man__ and then *whoops* Oh Lor-die well she gave me her hand. Be-cause
wheat in the bin__ and then *whoops* Oh Lord I was the fa-ther of twins. Be-cause
would-n't hes - i - tate I was *whoops* Oh Lord the grand - fa-ther of eight. Be-cause
trou-ble and pain__ but then *whoops* Oh Lor-die well I'd do it a - gain. Be-cause

Em   D   Bm7   Em   B7

she had__ kiss-es sweet-er than wine____ She had um um__

Em   Bm7   Em   B7   Em

2 3 & 4

kiss-es sweet-er than wine_____ sweet-er than wine._____

3. Well we
4. Well our
5. Well

Bm7   Em   Bm7   Em   B7

5

molto rit   *ad lib*   *fading out*

kiss-es sweet-er than wine._____

molto rit   *colla voce*   *morendo (dying away)*   *pp*

Bm7   B7   Em   Bm7   Em   Bm7   Em   Bm7   E

99

OH! MY PA-PA

Words by: Geoffrey Parsons and John Turner
Music by: Paul Burkhard

when they en-cored ___ him so, He'd shout,"Eh là hopp, Eh là hopp, Eh là hopp,Eh là hopp,Eh là hopp,Eh là

hopp,Eh là hopp,Eh là hopp!" His mouth was so wide,and his nose was so red,Eh là hopp, Eh là hopp,Eh là hopp! He'd

climb up a lad-der and fall on his head,And tho' it would hurt him he'd laugh as he said, "Eh là hopp, Eh là hopp,

Eh là hopp, Eh là hopp,Eh là hopp,Eh là hopp,Eh là hopp,Eh là hopp,Eh là hopp,Eh là hopp,Eh là hopp!"

REFRAIN *(slowly with feeling)*

Oh! My Pa - pa, To me he was so won-der-ful, Oh! My Pa - pa, To

me he was so good. No one could be so gen-tle and so lov-a-ble,

Oh! My Pa - pa, He al-ways un-der-stood. Gone are the days when

he would take me on his knee, And with a smile he'd change my tears to

laugh-ter. Oh! My Pa-pa, So fun-ny, so a-dor-a-ble, Al - ways the

clown, So com-ic in his way, Oh! My Pa-pa, To me he was so

won-der-ful, Deep in my heart I miss him so to - day.

- day. _____ Oh! My Pa - pa, _____ Oh! My Pa - pa. _____

PASSING STRANGERS

Words by: Mel Mitchell
Music by: Rita Mann

ve - ry strange. The hands I used to touch don't ev - en wave hel - lo.

C+7 C7 Fm7 Bb7 Eb Cm

How I miss your kiss, you'll nev - er know. _____ If you would on - ly

Am7(5b) D7(9b) Gm F#° Bb7 Eb

turn to me, speak my name, just once more, You might find right there and then,

Fm7 Bb7 Ab Eb 7b E° Fm7 Bb7 Eb C+7 C7

1.
stran - gers can be lov - ers a - gain.

2.
We gain. _____

Ab Fm7 (sus Eb) Eb Bb13 Bb+7 Bb7 Eb

TOO YOUNG

Words by : Sylvia Dee
Music by : Sid Lippman

SECRET LOVE

Words by : Paul Francis Webster
Music by : Sammy Fain

REFRAIN : Moderately, *with much tenderness*

VERSE

No - bod-y knew, not e - ven you; When I first start-ed walk-ing on wings;

But how long can a man or wo-man ev - er hope to hide Love that's lock'd up in-

-side? Ev'-ry sto-ry worth the spin-ning Must have a be - gin-ning.

REFRAIN: Moderately, *with much tenderness*

LOVE IS A MANY-SPLENDOURED THING

Words by : Paul Francis Webster
Music by : Sammy Fain

REFRAIN
Moderato (not too fast)

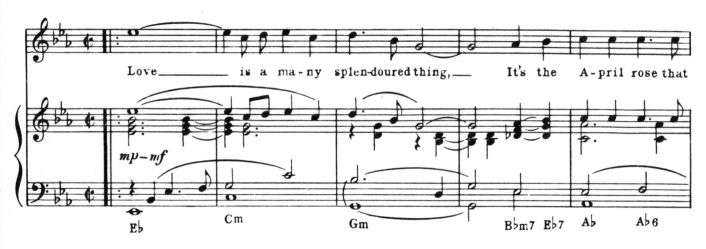

Love_____ is a ma-ny splen-doured thing,___ It's the A-pril rose that

on - ly grows in the ear - ly spring;___ Love is na-ture's way of giv-ing a

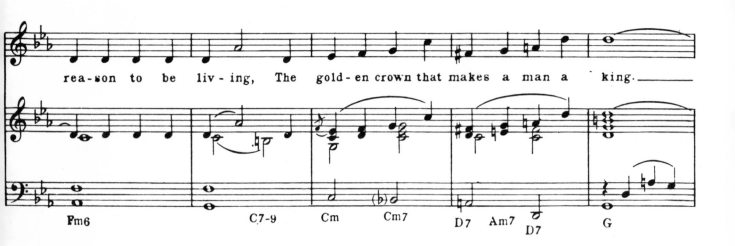

rea-son to be liv-ing, The gold-en crown that makes a man a king.____

Once _____ on a high and wind-y hill, ___ In the morn-ing mist two lov-ers kissed and the world stood still, ___ Then your fin-gers touched my si-lent heart and taught it how to sing, Yes, true Love's ___ a ma-ny splendoured thing. ___ thing. ___

VOLARE

Italian Words by: D. Modugno and F. Migliacci
English Words by: Mitchel Parish
Music by: Domenico Modugno

REFRAIN Moderato

Vo - la - re, ___ oh, oh! ___ Can - ta - re, ___ oh, oh, oh, oh! ___ Let's
Vo - la - re, ___ oh, oh! Can - ta - re, ___ oh, oh, oh, oh! ___ nel

fly way up to the clouds, A - way from the mad-den-ing crowds; We can sing in the glow of a
blu, di-pin-to di blu, fe - li - ce di sta - re las sù. E vo-la-vo, vo-la-vo fe-

star that I know of, Where lov-ers en-joy peace of mind, Let us leave the con-fu-sion and
-li - ce più in al - to del so-le ed an-co-ra più su, men-tre il mon-do pian pia-no spa-

WONDERFUL, WONDERFUL DAY

Words by: Johnny Mercer
Music by: Gene de Paul

mer - ry,   air - y   fair - y land.   And   so........ you'll for-give   me......
Go - in'   slow -'n',   grow-in' things.   Big   love........ for   my   dar - lin'

F#dim   Gm   Gm7   C7   F6   Fmaj7

...... if I   sim - ply   throw out   my   chest   and   say: Beau - ti - ful,
...... as we   share what - ev - er   may   come   our   way:

Cm7   F7-9   Bbmaj7   Eb7   Fmaj7

glo - ri - ous, heav - en - ly,   mar - vel - ous,   Won - der - ful, won - der - ful   day........

Gm7   Fmaj7   Gm7   Fmaj7   Gm7   C7   F

Won - der - ful   day........

cresc

Dm   Gm7   C7   Gm7   F   Gm7   F6

WHISPER WHILE YOU WALTZ

Words by : Christopher Hassall
Music by : Harry Parr Davies

All the torch-es are bright a - gain.

Tell all the fid - dles to play.

Though they rev - el a - round us,

Love is a world on its own.____

What do we care for the danc - ing crowd?

We shall be danc - ing a - lone.____

123

take me in your arms, And let the mus - ic keep twirl - ing us

round, And all a - round and still a - round._____

Whis - per the words that you love me Whis - per your

love while you waltz._____ waltz._____

Ain't Misbehavin' – Ain't She Sweet – Ain't That A Grand And Glorious Feeling
Am I Wasting My Time On You – Among My Souvenirs – Babette
Baby Face – Carolina Moon – Charmaine – Chicago
Dinah – Don't Bring Lulu – Five Foot Two, Eyes Of Blue
Girl Of My Dreams – Glad-Rag Doll – Happy Days And Lonely Nights
I Can't Give You Anything But Love – I'll Be With You In Apple Blossom Time – I'm Just Wild About Harry
It Had To Be You – Last Night On The Back Porch – Manhattan
Mistakes – My Blue Heaven – Nobody's Sweetheart
Pasadena – Ramona – Second Hand Rose
Shine – Side By Side – Singing In The Rain
S'posin' – Stumblin' – Sweetheart Of All My Dreams
That's My Weakness Now – Toot Toot Tootsie! (Goo'Bye) – Way Down Yonder In New Orleans
When You're Smiling – Who's Sorry Now? – You Were Meant For Me

A Bench In The Park – A-Tisket A-Tasket – Auf Wiedersehen My Dear
Back To Those Happy Days – Basin Street Blues – Between The Devil And The Deep Blue Sea
Blue Moon – Careless Love – Exactly Like You – For All We Know
Harbour Lights – Have You Ever Been Lonely? – I Can Dream Can't I?
Ida! Sweet As Apple Cider – I Only Have Eyes For You – I Surrender, Dear
It Happened In Monterey – It's Foolish But It's Fun – Lady Of Spain
Lazybones – Little White Lies – Love Is The Sweetest Thing
Lovely Lady – Lullaby Of Broadway – Marta
Memories Of You – Mood Indigo – Once In A While
On The Sunny Side Of The Street – Red Sails In The Sunset – Serenade In The Night
So Deep Is The Night – Song Of The Dawn – Sophisticated Lady
Star Dust – Stormy Weather – Sweet and Lovely – The Clouds Will Soon Roll By
When It's Sleepy Time Down South – Who's Taking You Home To-night?

The world went back to war in the Nineteen Forties. As usual the troops, and the families and friends they left behind, had music to keep them company. Love songs, torch songs, songs to help you remember and some to help forget. And when it was all over, there were songs to help in the celebrations. These are a few of the greatest.

Almost Like Being In Love – Always In My Heart – A Nightingale Sang In Berkeley Square
Brazil – Chattanooga Choo-Choo – Clipin Clopant
Coming In On A Wing And A Prayer – Deep In The Heart Of Texas – Down In The Glen
Elmer's Tune – Fascination – Frenesi – Granada
(The Gang That Sang) Heart Of My Heart – How Green Was My Valley – I'll Close My Eyes
I Should Care – Jealousy – Laura – Lazy River
Lilli Marlene – Maria Elena – Moonlight Serenade
My Guy's Come Back – My Heart And I – Now Is The Hour – Old Shep
Our Love Affair – Paper Doll – Perfidia – Perhaps, Perhaps, Perhaps
Red Roses For A Blue Lady – The Breeze And I – The Gypsy
We'll Keep A Welcome – White Cliffs Of Dover – You Are My Sunshine
You Belong To My Heart – You're Nobody 'Til Somebody Loves You – Yours

Printed in Great Britain by
St Edmundsbury Press, Bury St Edmunds, Suffolk